Your life is about to change very soon.

Can you feel it?

You have a goal you want to accomplish in life—to become the person you have always wanted to be! You know that your college experience is going to be a crucial and unforgettable part of this wonderful journey! And you picked up this book in the hope that it will help you get to where you want to go—the university you have always dreamed of attending, a place where you'll make wonderful friends, live an exciting college life, open doors to bright opportunities...maybe even find that special someone.

You're right.

You can have it all in college. When I was in college, I made many amazing friends from all over the globe, enjoyed living in a different city and being independent from my parents, and learned much more at college in 1 year than I did in all 4 years of high school combined. I got crystal clear about what I want to do after college, and landed a job with the best company in an industry I wanted to work in (clean energy). Oh yes, there were plenty of romances, too! My college experience shaped WHO I AM TODAY. Best of all, I got to attend my *dream college*.

I am here because I want you to have it too. You will simply miss WAY TOO MUCH if you don't experience the *dream college life* you deserve. I am giving you the very best, most cutting-edge tools to enable you to write an application essay that will dramatically increase your chances of being accepted into your dream college – whether it's Harvard, UCs, or Ivy League colleges.

However, I understand that the PROCESS of getting into colleges can be torturous.

When I first started my college application, my grades and SAT scores were so low that ALL my counselors, teachers, and friends not only thought that I wouldn't get accepted by my *dream college,* but that I wouldn't even make it into a mediocre college!

One of their favorite lines was: "I don't want to discourage you, but..."

However, despite their sincere effort to "not discourage me", I was very discouraged!

I couldn't sleep well at night. I kept thinking thought about my dim future. I imagined that I would never have my college experience at my dream college and would never become the person I wanted to be. I could almost see my parents' disappointed looks when I failed to get accepted.

I felt the doors of job opportunities closing as I settled for a lesser college. I could tell that my friends were saying, "I knew you couldn't do it!" and laughing behind my back.

Finally, one day, I'd had it!

I went on a journey searching for another way to get into colleges without good grades or SAT scores!

That's when I discovered something fascinating.

There was a group of students who didn't have the best grades, test scores, extracurricular activities, or even "family connections", but who got into Ivy League schools such as Harvard, Princeton, Yale, etc. The strange thing was, they had a "B" average and SAT scores below 1450! How could this be?

Naturally, I went to "investigate" these special students to discover their "secrets".

At first, no one wanted to tell me anything. But as I was particularly "persistent" in my approach, eventually they each showed me what they'd done that was different.

Then something fascinating emerged.

There was one thing all of these students had in common.

Somehow, their essays had impressed the college admissions judges so much that the judges felt **emotionally compelled** to accept them!

How could this be true? I didn't believe it! The college representatives never came to my campus and said, "As long as you do ABC in your application essay, we will admit you, even if you don't have good grades."

In disbelief, I went to talk to college admissions judges themselves, including Ivy League school admissions departments from Harvard,

Columbia, and other popular schools such as UCLA. I asked them, "You look at hundreds of application every day. How do you decide which ones to accept? What are the keys that make an application stand out and therefore get accepted by you?"

Again, the usual answers I got at first were, "We look at all aspects of the applicant, including grades, SAT scores, their extracurricular activities …"

But I didn't come all that way to listen to pre-rehearsed talks, so I pressed on. I showed them a long list of students who'd gotten in but who didn't have those things. "These students clearly do not have the best grades, fancy test scores, or engage in any impressive extracurricular activities. Their letters of recommendations are from normal teachers, and their families have no connection to your school. Why are they getting accepted instead of numerous other students who had better grades and SAT scores?"

What happened next was mind-blowing.

Most of them thought about it, and said, in effect, "Look, I read hundreds of applications **per day**. For schools like ours, we constantly get applicants with good grades and SAT scores, and they all look the same. After reading the first 2 hours of applications, my brain felt scrambled like an egg! Do you expect me to tell the difference between one applicant and the other pile of 170 applications?"

"The only reason I would accept someone is that if I can really **see from his essay** that he is someone who should be here, who must be here! He genuinely impresses me. In those cases, their grades and test scores don't matter."

With that knowledge, I went on a journey in search of techniques and methods for writing a college application essay that would get anyone, even me, into a great school without great grades or SAT scores.

I went to every single college presentation, talked to every college admissions judge I could find, and learned from every person I knew who had succeeded getting accepted to a top college without high grades or SATs.

I learned Neuro-Linguistic Programming to understand the psychological effects of different words, sentence structures, and syntax on a person.

I looked at hundreds of essays written by people who were accepted into top colleges with non-stellar GPAs or SATs.

I even sought techniques from a Master Hypnotherapist.

I learned techniques and a method to write the same application essay that only the top applicants wrote, consciously or unconsciously.

During this journey, I discovered 3 crippling myths that prevent almost all students from writing an outstanding essay!

Before I show you what they are, I want to tell you that almost ALL students believe the same myths – and if you did too, it's not your fault.

And...there is hope!

By reading this, you will learn the 3 crippling myths that most students are unaware of.

3 Crippling Myths about College Application Essays:

Crippling myth #1

Good grades and test scores are the only things that matter in my admissions. If I don't have good grades or test scores, my essay will make no difference.

This one really makes me seethe with anger, because it's 100% false.

I used to believe that if I didn't have good grades or SAT scores, the college would reject me, regardless of what I wrote in my college application essay.

After talking to more than a dozen college admissions judges from California to Massachusetts, I discovered that this belief is completely false!

GPA and test scores can only give approximate statistics of your current knowledge and income level.

Different schools' standards are vastly different. An "A" doesn't really mean anything if I can put 1/10th the effort and still get the same grade from a different school, or a different teacher.

Even though there is a list of the top 1000 high schools, it's impossible for the admissions staff to memorize them.

Your SAT/ACT test scores predict your income level more than your knowledge, simply because poor people can't afford Prince Reviews tutors.

These statistics hit a plateau when a few thousand candidates have the same high grades and SAT scores.

Top universities like Harvard are inundated with applicants with high grades and SATs every year. For them, high grades and SATs are not rare, eye-catching commodities.

These schools look for applicants who can bring something other than grades to the table.

And that is what you can show admissions judges in your College Application Essay!

If you, my friend, don't demonstrate the qualities that make the Admission Judges say, "He/she has what it takes!" – then expect a heartbreak when your decision letter comes!

That's why I'm going to show you, step-by-step, how to write essays that will blow the Admission Judge's mind!

And you won't learn this method anywhere else, because I am the only one teaching it.

So read on!

Crippling Myth #2

I can't write a good College Application Essay because I don't enough stellar experiences to write about.

Most counselors and college representatives stress that to write a great essay, you need a dazzling experience, or what I call a "Hollywood Experience".

Let me tell you a personal story.

When I was in my junior and senior years, many of my friends started playing a sport or joining a club or the school band.

When I asked them why they had suddenly developed the interest in those sports or clubs, they told me that they were doing all those activities so they could put something in their college applications.

Due to fear, I too joined the track-and-field team in the hope of having some positive/unique experience to describe in my college application essay.

How pathetic!

I was doing something I hated just to fake a meaningful experience in order to beg for admission to a school—and the experience itself wasn't even that unique!

What's worse, my later research found no correlation between the "fanciness" of the experience and the quality of an essay! What a waste of my life that was!

When someone tries to impress, get validation from, or win the college over by doing extracurricular activities they secretly hate, As a consequence, they start to chase validation from their dream college like a puppy. The Admission Judges can easily see that. And we all know where that leads.

To succeed, you need to convey here that you are the PRIZE.

Colleges are attracted to students who establish themselves as the PRIZE in the interaction.

They want to feel that you're so valuable that they must have you!

FACT: What colleges look for in a student's experience is not how "badass" or "unique" your experience is.

There is a fill-in-the-blank section where you can fill in your top achievements.

Colleges want to know "who YOU are" by the way you act and interpret your experience.

In a well-written essay, your personality, qualities, and characters communicate themselves to the Admission Judges so well that the essay will cause the Admission Judges to feel an emotional compulsion to grant you acceptance.

That is what gets those people into Harvard without top grades or SAT scores!

But, some say, "I haven't had any experiences that showed my awesome character!"

Wrong! Everyone's life is a bestselling book. Everyone's life is a #1 movie script. It just hasn't been written yet. In this book, we're going teach you how to choose your own life experience, one that will write the bestselling book that will create the way into the Admission Judges' hearts.

In this book, I will reveal to you my Entire Step-by-Step method of how to choose non-fancy material that demonstrates your best qualities so that Admission Judges will be emotionally

compelled to ACCEPT you into their college.

Crippling Myth #3

Only people with exceptional writing skills write great college application essays. I am not a good writer, so I can't write a good application essay.

I am sick and tired of hearing, "You have to show you're good writer by using a sophisticated vocabulary", "You need to demonstrate your academic level by using complicated grammar", or "Throw in SAT words so you sound more sophisticated."

Let me clarify something. Even achieving all of these things does not necessarily guarantee that the Admissions Judges will think you are sophisticated or ready to attend their college.

PLUS, an English major is only one of the major that most universities offer...if it's offered at all.

All those special people I know who got into Harvard without exceptional grades are not the ones who did the best in English class. However, they are GREAT COMMUNICATORS.

Most people don't talk to each other the way they write in "advanced" writing. We think those people who do are weirdos.

There is one, and only one, purpose for your College Application Essay—
TO GET YOU INTO YOUR DREAM COLLEGE THROUGH COMPELLING
COMMUNICATION WITH THE ADMISSIONS JUDGE.

Those special students didn't write complex words in their essays. They
communicated with the Admission Judges in a crystal-clear way about their
uniqueness, character, and what they could offer.

If you don't normally talk or write using complex sentence structures or
SAT words, forcing them into your essay will only hinder your
communication.

You don't need to write in a language that normal humans can't
understand just to impress an Admission Judge.

If you did, your essay would probably never be the one that really stands
out from the crowd.

Lesser colleges may accept you because they want someone who has
better English skills than the rest of the alcoholic idiots they have (and we all
know which schools those are)!

If you only want to learn how to get acceptance from average colleges
that are very easy to get into, then you don't need this book, and you don't
need to spend money on a "how-to" product.

Just attain their average grades and SAT scores, and you're almost guaranteed acceptance.

I don't know about you...but I only care about real success, with my dream college!

If you weren't aware of these myths, don't feel bad. There was a time when I wasn't aware of them, either.

Just 2 weeks before the deadline for my application, I finally combined all the techniques of writing an application essay I discovered into a method that would drastically increase the chances of anyone getting accepted by a top college.

I used that method myself – and sure enough, I got accepted by my *dream college*. (It was Babson College, ranked #1 in Entrepreneurship in the world for the past 25 years. Even though it has a relatively high acceptance rate of 26% compared with Ivy Leagues schools, my grades and SAT scores made ME a very unlikely candidate to get into Babson. So it was a big deal for someone like me to get in.)

What's more, this experience inspired me to explore exactly what cracks the **College Admissions Code**.

For the next 3 years, I dedicated my time to traveling across the U.S. to perfect this method.

I read every single book on college admissions I could, consulted with counselors from numerous private college prep firms, went to about 60 different college presentations, and met one-on-one with more than 30 different college admissions judges.

I traveled, visited, and learned from everyone from Harvard College admissions judges to psychologists.

I found and learned from "Bests" who got into top schools only because they wrote outstanding college application essays.

After a while, the pattern became obvious.

There is a specific set of triggers which, when applied in a student's essay, will drastically increase his chances of getting acceptance to any top university. These are not difficult techniques – in fact, they are relatively simple to apply. But because how uncommon they are, most people don't know them, and wouldn't normally think of them.

In 2016, I condensed the techniques into a writing process that will make a student's college application instantaneously 10 times more powerful.

I call it the Dream College Acceptance Method.

Even though this is not an end-all, be-all method that would "save everyone" and guarantees everyone to get into anywhere if they have absolute "D" or "F" grades and truly lousy SAT scores, it will DRASTICALLY increase the quality of your college application essay and tremendously improve your chances of getting accepted.

In fact, once you finish this book and do all the exercises, your essay WILL be at least 10 times more effective and powerful than the all rest of the applicants who are competing with you.

There is a catch, though.

The catch is that you need to make a choice, right now.

This book contains the most powerful tactics for writing an undergraduate college application essay. But we all know that buying a book alone is not what will get you into your dream college. YOU must be the person who gets you into your dream college!

Will you finish the book, take all the action steps and use all the powerful tactics you're going to learn to develop an outstanding essay that will bring you to your dream college?

If you want to write essays like other average students, if you want to settle for less, then I respect your choice - and I understand. Close the book now, and get a refund.

However, if you are not afraid to leap into the greatness of your future; if you want to utilize the most powerful and cutting-edge tactics from Neuro-Linguistic Programming to English Linguistic Skills; if you are willing to write an outstanding essay that will bring you to your dream college,

Then make a decision right now that you are going to put in 100% effort and commitment. You will use what this book teaches you, and you will do whatever it takes to write your very best, life-changing College Application Essay!

How to Use this Book

Congratulations! By committing yourself, you are now among the top 1% of applicants who take action to write a phenomenal essay that blows Admission Judge's minds and brings you to your dream college! (We are going to abbreviate Admission Judges as "AJ". Also, most of them are female, so we will use "she" when I refer to them.)

A quick note on how to use the book effectively to get the most out of it:

Read the book as if you are listening to a speech. Do not overthink. Be relaxed and receptive. If your mind gets too tense, you can't be receptive to information. Follow each action step at the end of each key section. The action steps are designed to be easy and completed with ease. It is crucial to do the action steps! They are what will ultimately help you make a difference in your essay.

While you are reading this book, have a pencil/pen, a piece of paper or a notebook with you at all time. If you get a "spark" in the middle of reading, close the book and start writing! It doesn't matter what you write or if they are just messy ideas. Write them all down until you run out of stuff to write! This is called a "capture". Empty your brain, and then resume reading.

The ideas and passages you write down will help you later when you're writing your essay, for they are likely to be amazing ideas that will make all the difference.

When you write your essay by following the action steps in this book, you are likely to get into a flow, feeling as if the essay is writing itself. When this happens, let it flow, and do not interrupt. The best art creates itself.

When you are reading this book or writing your essay, turn off any distractions such as cellphones and e-mail alerts, if possible. Studies have shown that if a person gets interrupted, it takes 20 minutes just to return to the same level of focus.

Finally, each person has picked up this book for different reasons. However, your focus in this book is on yourself. Take a minute right now and ask yourself: what do YOU want out of this book? Do you want to learn what to write in your application essay? Do you want to learn techniques that will make your application look better?

You may not know all of the answers, but at least think of a few outcomes you want from this book. Now, this is important: write down in your notebook why you absolutely MUST write the best essay possible to get into your dream college. Also write down what you want to get out of this book.

This is very important. As you are reading, if you have a strong reason and a clear outcome, your brain will search for answers as you read this book, and you will be more likely achieve your outcome. Go ahead! Write them down if you haven't. I will wait.

As you're reading the book, focus on YOUR outcome as we work together. This is a key step. Do not skip it! If you don't know how to do it, imagine you've finished the book. Imagine that this is the end of the book, you have finished reading and doing the exercises. What are you leaving with? What do you want to leave with?

Once you have done that, move on to the first chapter.

Contents

Chapter 1 20

Chapter 2 35

Chapter 3 41

Chapter 4 49

Magic Bullets Set One 58

Chapter 5 71

Chapter 6 77

Chapter 7 89

Chapter 8 94

Magic Bullets Set Two 98

Last Words 109

Chapter 1
What Colleges Want

What do you look for in your romantic partner? A warm smile? An extraordinary personality? A nice butt?

All three?

What if that the person you are attracted to doesn't have any of things you like? Would you still be attracted to them?

Universities have a set of qualities they look for in applicants, too. If you don't demonstrate to colleges the things they look for, do you think the colleges will be attracted to you?

So which qualities will turn colleges on? (Especially your dream college!)

According to the Pareto's Principle, the 80/20 rule, 20% of the effort makes 80% of the difference. Using the boy/girl example, qualities that turn boys on are likely big boobs and tight butts in a girl. About 80% (if not 120%) of instantaneous attraction comes from those 2 things alone.

It turns out that, out of thousands of "qualities" out there, a few qualities compose 80% of what the colleges are looking for as well. These qualities are the leverage points that make you particularly attractive to colleges. They are also the qualities that get the Admission Judges' (AJ) attention the most while they are reading your essay. Demonstrating these trigger qualities for college essays will give you a huge edge over all other applicants.

After much investigation, I found that there are 7 key qualities that colleges look for the most. I call them *The 7 Fundamental Qualities*.

The 7 Fundamental Qualities

1. Integrity

This is the most important quality, so it's at the top of the list!

Think of all the students in your school you know. If you can no longer be yourself and have the power to choose to become one of the persons in your school, who will you choose to be?

Now, same scenario. But this time, think of the person that you ABSOUTELY do not want to become. Who is that? This should be an easier one.

Now think about why you want to become the first person, but not the second. What quality in that first person do you admire? And what quality in the second person do you despise? List these qualities, if necessary.

If you are totally honest, the first person, among many other good qualities, must, above all, possess integrity. If he/she is a lying, backstabbing, dishonest person, the chances are that you won't want to be like him/her.

The second person, the one you absolutely despise, although they may have multiple negative qualities, their lack of integrity is probably the one that repulses you the most.

The importance of integrity becomes increasingly important as you grow older. What would happen when the wrong people become business people, politicians, or doctors? When a college admits a person who lacks integrity, it often brings severe damage to the college in a variety of ways. This person will make other students/faculty's experience unpleasant, and most likely damage the college's reputation in the future.

Therefore, the number-one quality that colleges look for is Integrity.

2. Standards

What truly makes a difference in a person's life?

If we examine this question closely, it is his *Standards*. When a person has a high standard – for example, for grades – he will never allow his grades to fall below a certain point. Yes, once a while he may not "make it", but you can bet that his average grade is much higher than others because of his high standards.

Everyone has a standard for everything; for his health, for his relationships, for his finances, etc. And the person's standard determines his life.

So what is a *standard*?

A *Standard* is something that you MUST have, not SHOULD have. You see, we rarely get our "should", but we always get our "musts".

If someone is overweight, it is rarely the case that that person has a high standard for his body. If a person has a high standard for his body, he would eat in certain ways, exercise in certain ways, and even sleep in certain ways! The same goes for any other areas of one's life.

Colleges know that ONLY students with high standards in life will succeed in and after college. In addition, *the way a person does anything tends to be the way a person does everything*. Students with high standards in life are the ones who achieve high grades, treat others with respect, and, frankly, get the best jobs after college. If you do not know the areas in life where you have high standards, simply look at those areas where you have achieved outstanding results. Only outstanding standards produce outstanding results.

3. Drive

As much as we are focusing on GETTING INTO colleges at this moment, getting into a college – or even the college experience itself – are not our ultimate goal. We all have a goal, a life, and a career that we will pursue after college. College is merely a stepping-stone to something bigger and greater. AJs know this well (because they lived it) and keep this in mind when they read application essays.

Drive is *the emotional fuel a person uses to strive to one definite outcome*. Drive is not accepting any other possibilities except the one you've set and taken definite action to achieve. Drive means following what you believe in. It can be as small as fulfilling a pinky-promise, or as big as the president's promise of reducing American unemployment by 10% in 3 years.

Students who are driven in college always do better than students who are uncertain and lingering. Graduates who are driven and describe their goals in writing makes more money than the rest of the graduate class combined in 10 years. Applicants who are driven and certain about which dream college they want to attend always have much better chances of success than the ones who are uncertain where they want to go.

Driven people have a strong sense of certainty and take a lot more action to become successful in both college and life. It doesn't mean that driven students always get what they want. It simply means that the uncertain students don't know what they want, and always get what life throws to them.

The AJ knows what's going to happen if he accepts a driven kid. The kid is going strive, get the best out of their college experience and beyond. The AJ also knows what will happen if he accepts an uncertain kid. The kid is likely to drop out, change college, or become unemployed for a while after graduation. Successfully demonstrating that you are driven will prove your worthiness to enter the university before they even consider your other qualities.

You have things in your life you are driven to do. Maybe it is reaching a new level in a hobby (or video game). Maybe it is helping a specific person, or maybe it is winning a competition. Show it to the AJ!

4. Resourcefulness

When you ask people, "Why haven't you achieve your goals yet?", what is the number-one response most people give?

"I don't have the money!"

"I don't have the time!"

"I don't have the connections!"

"I don't have a big _____!"

The answer is always a lack of RESOURCES. But we all know that the answer is not a lack of resources, don't we? The real answer is a lack of the quality known as RESOURCEFULNESS. If you are resourceful enough, can't you figure out a way to have investors put money to your business idea? If you are resourceful enough, can't you find extra time to work on your goals? If you are resourceful and a decent person, can't you find new friends who will assist you?

A College is a resource center as much as an educational institute.

The resources that most colleges offer range from study-abroad programs to career assistance. If the college accepts you, they want you to fully utilize the resources they offer. If a resourceful student wants to accomplish something in college, he/she will not only work hard, but will also work smart by utilizing the resources the colleges offers.

Effectively demonstrating the quality of RESOURCEFULNESS will make the judge believe that accepting you is the right choice. You are able to fully utilize the campus resources and get the best out of your college experience. Colleges want to create as much value for you as possible. Failing to demonstrate this quality will make the AJ think it is a waste to give you a spot in their college unless you are going to take advantage of the resources that the college offers.

5. Courage

Any honest college representative will tell you that despite many of the wonderful experiences you will have at their school, you are also going to encounter many uncomfortable moments and fears.

They could range from roommate problems to having that big interview for your next job. The biggest ones, perhaps, are the ones when you face an ethical dilemma in which doing the right and courageous thing seems to work against your self-interest. Most of these situations are very uncomfortable. When you use your courage to overcome fear, you grow. You become stronger and more mature each time you overcome fear, and you become more ready to handle what's coming next. Colleges need students who have courage and are able to handle what's going to be thrown at them in their college life. A person who doesn't get out of his comfort zone never excels.

To demonstrate the quality of courage, first we need to understand what courage is. Out of the numerous definitions I have heard, I think that the best written definition of courage is "feeling the fear of doing something, but acting in the face of fear."

Courage doesn't mean picking a fight with two men who are bigger than you, or piercing your body in places that other human beings don't want to know about! It is when you are afraid to death of singing in front of a live audience, but still perform at your school's talent show. It is when all your friends tell you that you can't do it, but you still accomplish the impossible! It is calling up someone who you wronged before and apologizing, despite your fear of embarrassment and shame.

Can you see the difference? Physically, it is much more difficult and dangerous to fight two bigger guys than to sing to a crowd – but the latter takes much more courage than the former. It is not about what you did that makes you courageous. It is feeling YOUR fear – and doing it anyway. It can be as easy (or as hard) as talking to the opposite sex.

Can you recall a particular event where you overcame a tremendous amount of fear to act on something you normally wouldn't do and grew as a person because of it? It may be your next essay topic!

6. Humor

Despite what you may have heard – "You don't need to be humorous in your application essay if you are not normally funny", or "You don't have to be funny", humor plays a particularly big role in the college application essay.

The college admission judge reads hundreds of essays a day. No matter how much the person likes to read, it does get a little boring, exhausting, or even a little excruciating after the first 6 hours of reading application essays. So even if humor is not the most important thing for an individual essay, it is a big deal when in the context of a judge who reads applications 8 hours a day, 5 days a week.

If you can get a laugh from a person, it does two things:

1. It relaxes them.

2. It puts them in a good mood.

Is it to your advantage if your judge is relaxed and in a good mood when she reads your essay?

Very much so!

Whenever a judge gets a smirk or laugh from your essay, she gets a break from all the boring essays that sound the same. You will have a real shot at him/her actually actively reading what you wrote...maybe even finishing your essay! If your essay can make a judge's day, she is going to like you. When a judge likes you, she is going to let you in.

"But I am not funny! What should I do?"

I have never met a single person in my life who never cracked me up at least once in our conversation! Have you EVER cracked up a friend? At least once? If you can make your friends laugh, you could do the same thing to college admission judges. Just relax, get into a good state, and let your thoughts flow.

7. The Ability to Genuinely Connect with Others

The ability to connect with another human being has been valued by all cultures throughout history. Real connections with a friend, a family member, or someone you just met enrich both you and the other person. It creates relationships among friends, business partners, families, and lovers.

Colleges know how important connection is for a student. **Every great thing you do in life, you do through other people.** In college you will meet people who will likely be lifelong friends, business partners, or mentors. By connecting with people, you both make yourself more successful and loved, and you contribute love to others.

Students with the ability to build great relationships make lots of friends in colleges, build relationships with professors and visitors whom they may later work for, create value for the school, and are likely to have jobs already lined up upon graduation.

Do you know someone, in your school perhaps, who is always alone and never talks to ANYONE? Is he/she normal? Do you want to be around that person? Do people see him/her as having a high social status – or as crazy? People like that in colleges will isolate themselves as well. They won't go out and take advantage of what the college offers. They won't make many friends. They will lose the opportunities in front of them because they don't connect with the key people. They waste their talents and gifts.

If you were the AJ, which type of student would you pick? The one who will connect with others and contributes to others' lives, or the one who isolates herself?

"But I am shy!"

It's okay if you're shy. Connection is not going out to a cocktail party and meeting a bunch of half-drunk people you don't care about. Connection is the real energy formed between two people when they both know that they care about each other. Have you ever talked to someone for a while and, in a moment, know that you've formed a connection? That is it.

You have people in your life right now you have a connection with. They may be your parents, siblings, friends, or mentors. The relationships you developed helped you in your essential growth. If you have done it before, you can do it in the future. So all you need to do in your college application essay (sometimes abbreviated as CAE) is to demonstrate that you have connections with existing friends/families/mentors.

Now you know the specific qualities that colleges look for and the reasons behind them. Now it's time to act and allow that knowledge to really give you the edge!

Action step 4

For each of the 5 qualities, search in your memory and write down examples of how your life experiences apply to that quality. Feel good as you compliment yourself!

Chapter 2
A Few Rules on Writing the College Application Essay

All rules can be broken and have exceptions. However, a few rules can make your life much easier when writing college essays. Following them can help you avoid some common and critical mistakes that a lot of applicants make.

1. Be Honest

There has always been an ethical dilemma that arises in many students' minds when they write their college application essays. The dilemma is, "I wonder if I can be a little 'ethically innovative' and 'exaggerate the truth' a bit to increase my chances of admission." An admissions counselor once told me, "This is probably the number-one mistake that applicants make. We can see clearly when a student is trying to make up a story or exaggerate anything. Whenever we see them, their applications automatically go where they belong – into the trash can."

Personally, I think that it simply takes too much energy to debate with myself about whether or not I should lie on my college application. The downside of being caught is too great. The effort doesn't pay off. Plus, if I do lie and get into the college, for the rest of my life I will always wonder whether I really deserved to be there.

If you write honestly, AJ will sense your honesty. This is a strong plus for you. A huge number of students think they can lie and get away with it. So do yourself a favor: just be honest and focus on writing the best essay with what you have, instead of scrambling your brain trying to make stuff up.

2. Don't write overly sexual stuff

I know. Some people are weird. I heard more than once from AJ about how he/she (usually a "she") got disgusted and uncomfortable when reading detailed sexual descriptions in some student essays. I really don't understand why someone would include their sex life in a College application essay.

I mean, you don't just go around and tell strangers about your sex life, right? (I hope not.) So why put them in your essay? If you're trying to turn the AJ on, just do it directly in the AJ's office! (Kidding!) In all seriousness, I know that they may have been particularly exciting experiences for you, but even the "Hippie Colleges' admissions" won't want to read about that.

3. Keep One Focus in Your Writing.

Have you ever talked to someone about a topic, but deviated from your main conversation and start talking about something else? By the time you were done, you forgot what you were originally trying to say?

Let's say you're trying to talk about a car you liked. You described how you saw that type of car in the park, then you start talking about the park, your first time in the park, and how you had a bad breakup in that park, then about that ex... then you suddenly realize you were supposed to be talking about the car!

People do the same things all the time in their essays. We are easily carried away by our wonderful storytelling skills. However, it is very time-consuming to return to focus after a deviation. So keep this in mind and check your essays to see if you have stayed focused.

4. Don't Lose Your Edge

When I first started to write my CAE, my friend Jason read it. "Wow, Shu," he said. "I can really see it's YOU who wrote the essay." My edgy personality was in between the sentences I wrote. Later I showed my essay to 3 English teachers, 2 counselors, and a stranger I met at a coffee shop named "Busters". Something interesting happened after the 5th edit in Busters. When my friends read my essay again, they could no longer tell that I had written it. The essay had more elaborate words and looked more pleasing to others. But somewhere along the line, my "edge" had vanished.

I finally decided, "You know what? I am going to screw some people's opinions and only listen to the 3 top people whose advice makes the most sense!" I went back and corrected some of my sentences and word choices – and my essay was back to "Shu wrote it".

No great individuals have ever pleased everyone. If you want to please everyone, you can't inspire anyone. A pleasing essay may come across as more politically correct or more sophisticated. But it is also boring. Your true personality gets killed in an essay that pleases everyone. So make your own smart choices. Listen to the top 3 bits of advice you hear and decide for yourself. Like my friend Zoe said, "Screw it! I will write the essay MY way!"

Zoe got into her first-choice college.

5. Stay Sane

It's not uncommon for an applicant to feel obligated to be "different" and "unique" so they come off sounding crazy in their essays...and they don't know it! They try too hard.

It is much easier for a college to refuse a student who sounds crazy in his essay than to kick an actual crazy student out. Being different is not being idiotic. It is entertaining to read a crazy essay once a while, but they serve no other purpose than entertainment. The judges will definitely reject applicants who seem crazy, but have no value to offer. So do yourself a favor: don't try too hard to be unique and come across like a crazy person! You're already unique. Just let your personality out. There is no need to TRY to be "unique"!

Chapter 3
Understanding the Topic

The First step in writing a College Application Essay that gives you an edge understands the topic correctly.

When we ask most people "where does the first stage of digestion take place?" The usual answer is, "The stomach!"

The fact is, the first stage of digestion starts with digestive enzymes (saliva) in a person's month.

When we ask the majority of students what the first step of writing a college application essay (CAE) is, the answer we get is always "write the introduction".

However, the first step starts way before that!

Fact: The first step in writing a successful CAE is **clearly understanding what the topics ask for**. No wonder so many students are having trouble on their CAEs!

Have you ever spent a lot of effort writing an essay, and later your teacher just end up giving you a bad grade because your essay doesn't really answer the prompt? (I know—that bitch!)

I had done the same many times myself! It is very frustrating every time because I spent all this time writing a good essay (or I thought!) but my grade and effort got screwed over because I didn't read the essay prompts carefully. Or I didn't understand what the topic was asking for!

What if this happens during your college application essay writing, do you think that the consequence may be a little bit more severe than getting a bad grade on a paper?

"Nah... I will never do that!" That's what most people say. Interesting, it just happens that those "most people" are the ones who make this particular mistake! During writing your college application essay, it is much easier to get pumped (or flooded with fear) and not pay full attention on what the essay topics ask for!

To write an essay that woos the AJ, you FIRST need to read the essay prompts/topics. It is important to understand the essay topics before going into the context!

An outstanding essay comes with an outstanding understanding of the topic.

Luckily for us, almost all undergraduate application essay topics mainly ask for one thing. It appears in various forms and ways asked by different colleges but the core of the questions is the same all across.

What?! Impossible! Really???

Really.

Different colleges have essay topics that APPEAR to be different from one another.

Here are some examples, read and see if you can find any commonalities:

1. Evaluate a significant experience, achievement, risk you have taken, or ethical dilemma you have faced and its impact on you.

2. A range of academic interests, personal perspectives, and life experiences adds much to the educational mix. Given your personal background, describe an experience that illustrates what you would

bring to the diversity in a college community, or an encounter that demonstrated the importance of diversity to you.

3. Tell us about a personal quality, talent, accomplishment, contribution or experience that is important to you. What about this quality or accomplishment makes you proud and how does it relate to the person you are?

4. Unusual circumstances in your life- Travel or living experiences in other countries

5. Using the statement below as a jumping off point, tell us about an event or experience that helped you define one of your values or changed how you approach the world. "Princeton in the Nation's Service" was the title of a speech given by Woodrow Wilson on the 150th anniversary of the University. It became the unofficial Princeton motto and was expanded for the University's 250th anniversary to "Princeton in the nation's service and in the service of all nations." Woodrow Wilson, Princeton Class of 1879, served on the faculty and was Princeton's president from 1902–1910.

6. Write about an event or experience that has deeply affected your development as a person.

7. In the space provided below, or on a separate sheet if necessary, please describe which activity (extracurricular and personal activities or work experience) has had the most meaning for you, and why.

8. Indicate a person who has had a significant influence on you, and describe that influence.

9. Discuss some issue of personal, local, national, or international concern and its importance to you.

10. Describe a character in fiction, a historical figure, or a creative work (as in art, music, science, etc.) that has had an influence on you, and explain that influence.

11. Describe the world you come from — for example, your family, community or school — and tell us how your world has shaped your dreams and aspirations

12. Pick a topic of your own choosing that will give you the opportunity to express to us a sense of how you think, what issues and ideas are most important to you, and a sense of your personal philosophy, traits, goals, etc.

Are you seeing the patterns? What do you think 80% of all the prompts ask? Take a moment and write it down. You can guess if you don't know. I will wait.

The topic can appear to ask you to tell them about "an academic interest, a personal perspective, an activity, an accomplishment, or a significant person". Take a closer look.

How did you develop your academic interest?

If you think hard, you developed an interest from an experience (or a series of experience over time) that changed the perspective of how he looks at that subject. There is a point in life where you had your first class on this subject, you had a good experience and you became interested, "yeah...I like this subject!" Or possibly, when you first skied, you liked it and decided to take it ever since.

How do you write about the significant person in your life? Do you describe him or her like a biography? Or do you write a specific EXPERIENCE you had with this person?

How do you illustrate your hobby/activity? Do you say "I run track for 3 years in high school. 10th grade, 11th grade, and 12th grade" Or do you write down a specific experience in your activity that is a "game changer" in your growth as a person?

My favorite tricky topic is "how your world has shaped your dreams and aspirations?"

Does a person's environment shape his character? Or does a person's choices of how to interact with his environment makes him who he is? Your "world" never defines you! There is only one person who can and ever will.

Now, the real question they are asking here is "Through your experience of interaction with your unique environment1, what decisions you have made that shaped you who you are today?"

I am giving you all these examples for you to see that most the essay topics points to writing "a specific experience" even they may appear to be letting you write something very different.

Sadly, too many students don't know the *real question* here and they go ahead to actually describing their "world". How their "world" shapes them instead of how they take charge of what their "world" throws to them...well, sucks for them!

When we look over all what types of essay topics colleges ask for, above 80% of the time, the CAE topics ultimately ask you for an experience. The goal is to discover your values, beliefs and how you act as a person through a core experience in your life that you grew from. Through your experience, you directly, clearly, and honestly show how you act as a person, your characters. You show your background, how you grow, how you interpret what something means, and how you contribute to other people's lives as a positive example. It is clear, direct, and leaves little room for other interpretations.

When you watch a movie, everything about the main character as a person becomes crystal clear in 2 hours. You don't need see his 60 years of life experience to conclude his characters. Who he is as a person is demonstrated clearly in 1 story of his life. Your uniqueness and character will be demonstrated quickly in your experience just like the main character of a movie...if it is well written! That's why the colleges like to know who you are through your experiences.

The rest 20% of the time, the CAE topics explore your values, characters, and believes through direct dialogues2 (such as "letter to roommate"), crazy topics (if you can be an ice cream, which flavor would you be?), and your opinions (what are some of the challenges facing the world at the dawn of the new millennium?).

There is a reason that these types of prompts are not used frequently over all.

It is very hard to go deep to discover you as a person by interpreting your dialogues, crazy scenarios, or opinions. We can understand a person deeply by his key experiences in life, but just by him talking about his opinions or telling what he would do in a crazy scenario, we can still get to know him...but not as deep. And it takes an exceptional writing skill to show who you are through this kind of dialogue essays.

We are going to focus on the experience type of topics in this book. According to Pareto's Principle – The 80-20 rule, experience type topics roughly appear 80% of the time. The rest kinds of topics appear 20% of the time. Experience topic is the majority of what you are going to focus on.

Also, to write an essay that will blow the judges away, we have to go deep. Opinions and crazy scenarios can be the bomb too! They can provide intellectual entertain the judges for a second but it is VERY RARE to find a truly outstand one that the judge is able to see the applicant's true personality. If you have a real genius idea about the crazy scenarios or opinions and you know for sure it is going to work, (not the ones that you think is genius but many others are writing similar things) GO FOR IT!

If you want to try using the experience one, do the quick exercise below

Action step 2:

Look at all your CAE topics and see if which one fits as "writing an experience" and how it fits. Write each one of them down in to *either the Experience Category* or *the Dialogue Category*.

Under each topic of the Experience Category, write down how this topic fits as an experience and what the prompt is asking. If you don't have CAE topics right now, use the above examples in this chapter. Enjoy, you may find something surprising.

Chapter 4
Choose Your Topic

How to choose what to write that put you into the top 1% application file

When I first started to write my college application essay, I wished that I have some incredible experiences that would woo the judges. So I started searching into my memory for incredible experiences.

However the result was disappointing.

1. I was never the captain of any sports team or won any chess competitions.

2. I never had any adventures that typically seen in films that change me as a person.

3. Worst of all, I never got a letter from an owe inviting me to Hogwarts, or met any vampires that gave me super powers.

So I guess I am a muggle and can't write about any extraordinary magical experiences.

That's not cool.

At this point, I had 2 choices:

1. Microwave spiders (therefore give them radiation) and have them bite me in hopes of becoming a human-mutant who uses his ability to fight crimes (or create crimes, which is a more likely scenario for me).

2. Actually write down something that may not seem fancy but deeply matters to me.

The first choice did not work for the spiders were hard to catch and kept dying in the microwaving process, I proceeded to the latter. To my surprise, the second choice is not only easier for me to write, but also what the Admission Judges want.

As we know now, choosing the key material to write down in your application is the foremost important step in starting to write the CAE.

Without the correct ingredients, the best chef cannot cook an average tasting meal. Without the correct material, the best writer's essay is going to suck. So what experience do you need to put down on your CAE that not only will win the judge's heart, but also makes it easier and more enjoyable for you to write?

If you are applying for undergraduate college right now, I assume that you are around 17 or 18 years old. You are not likely to have what I call "Hollywood Experiences" (Experiences that can only be obtained through a bat-mobile, Titanic, or Clooney)

Trying to come up an experience that "impresses" the judge is not going to get you anywhere...because every single other applicant is doing it! They try to exaggerate how great their experiences are. Some even fabricate those experiences. Believe or not, after a while they sound quite the same. With years of experience, the AJs can see through the "Hollywood-wanna-be experiences" like how a non-American can see through the competency of Sarah Palin.

So what experience do I use then?

It is simple:

Write an experience that made a KEY difference in YOUR life.

And the secret is:

It's not about WHAT you write; it's HOW you write it.

Colleges want to see "who YOU are" by the way you act in and interpret your experience. In a well written essay, your personalities, qualities, and characters communicate themselves to the AJ so well that it will trigger the AJ to feel an emotional compulsion to grant you acceptance.

"Who you are" is the actions you habitually and consistently take and will be taking in the future which would ultimately lead you to a destination.

Our ultimate destination in life is shaped by the effects of our daily habitual and consistent actions. Every action has a cause. If the action is one that you habitually perform, it has a strong cause. Strong causes are beliefs we form during few STRONG KEY EXPERIENCES in our lives.

If you try to remember, there are experiences in your life that caused you to believe in certain way, or in another word, make a neuro-association.

When my friend Nick really liked a girl in 10th grade, he dated her and poured his heart. Then one day, he found out that the girl was cheating on him for over 2 months! Of course he got very angry! But he also made a critical neuro-association in his mind at that moment: if I get too emotionally close to the point of trusting the girl, I am going to get hurt. So, I am not going to trust anyone!

He had a key experience. He made an association: Trusting someone = ultimate pain

Even though his belief is completely untrue, the neuro-association was very strong. So in the years followed, he never got emotionally close to any girl he dated, and he actually never trusted anyone! He never made a single new close friend since then; and he was rejected from numerous jobs because he came off as a depressed and cold person in the interviews. Imaging how depressed and lonely living a life like that!

The direction of his life was not shape by "big" events such as not messed up in a job interview, or blew his chance to find his love of life...It was shaped by that one emotional experience in 10th grade! And he was not even aware of it!

So how does this relate to choosing my material for CAE?

Can you notice how certain types of experiences in your life that happened and after that experience you made decisions that altered your future behaviors?

Those experiences are what I call "key experiences". Key experiences tend to be very strong. You interpret what this experience mean to you and form new believes. Once you have the new believes, your identity changes. So does that mean experience itself is what matters?

No. two people can have the exact same experience and but put different meanings to the same experience, and have different outcomes in life.

Tony Robbins, one of the most successful Entrepreneur and inspirational speaker alive, was very poor when he was young. In fact, he was so poor that on Thanks Giving day, there was no food! While his mother was fighting with his father about the fact that there is nothing for the family to eat, there was a sudden knock on the door.

Some stranger brought food to Tony's family!

Tony's father saw this action by this stranger and thought "what does this mean? This is Charity! I can't take care of my family!" He made an association: My financial incompetence = not able to take care of the family. So what should I do? I should leave my family. And that's what he did.

Tony however, had a completely different association from the same experience! Tony thought "first of all, there is food! What a treat!" His little heart was filled with joy and started to enjoy the food. Then he made a very important neuro-association that affected the rest of his life.

"What does this mean?" Tony asked himself. "Strangers care about me, so I care about strangers".

So when Tony was 17 in high school and had enough money, he went to feed 2 families during Thanks Giving. It was the most fun thing he did in his life! Also most moving experience he ever had. Next year, he fed 4 families. Next year 8! After 8 Tony thought "Shit I could use some help!" So he got his friend involved, he grew 11 companies, he built a foundation. 18 years later, Tony Robbins Foundation fed 2 million people through 35 countries all during holidays.

Now you see, Tony and his father both had the exact same experience. They don't have food on Thanks Giving. A stranger knocked on the door and delivered free groceries.

The difference is they made different meanings from that emotional experience. Tony's father's meaning of that experience is "My financial incompetence = not able to take care of the family." Tony's is "strangers care about me = I care about strangers".

They both took actions caused by the meanings they give to the same event. And the ultimate destinations of their lives were directed by the effects of their actions. Tony's father died and no one in his family besides Tony went to his funeral. Tony became one of the world's most famous entrepreneur and speaker.

You have moments in your life where you made meanings that shaped your habitual actions in the past, is shaping your actions at the present, and will be shaping your actions in the future if you decide to keep those meanings. The phrase "Who you are" colleges are looking for is not WHAT experiences you had; it's HOW you interpreted your key experiences. It is the WHY you do what you do and will keep doing them in the future.

AJs may not consciously know the detailed psychology behind it the way I just showed you. But they know that the key meanings you made in your key experiences in life shift your mindset and makes you are, and who you will be.

Can you think back of an experience you had, you made meanings and decisions during that experience, and you positively grew from that experience?

There is nothing more convincing to colleges than showing them what key experience you had, what associations you made, and what specific actions you took after that. They will know exactly your characters, your background, how you grow, how you interpret what something means, and how you interact with other people and contribute in their lives.

Most students never know this concept; they thought they could just write a seemingly glamorous experience that they don't truly care about. Their "who you are" don't show at all.

So the essay becomes another trophy experience essay like the first 999 trophies the AJ read. They not only lose the only opportunity to inspire the AJ through their application essay, they also wasted the AJ's time.

AJs hate to waste time.

What if my experience is a "bad experience" and I made negative associations that are hurting my life right now! What should I do? The event that you perceive as "bad events" could become empowering events. Tony Robbins' father definitely perceived the event of strangers give my family food as "the ultimate proof of failure in life" yet the same event empowered Tony. So it was not the event that was bad. It was what you focused during that emotional moment and what you made it mean.

If you realize that your limiting belief and unproductive association is counterproductive and hurting your life. Don't write it down in your essay! Change the meaning of it into an empowering meaning and don't tell the AD about the story of how the negative meanings you formed such as witnessing your friend getting shot in the neighborhood by gangs from certain racial group so you made the association of all the people in that racial group are demons and you dedicated the past 3 years killing off those people.

Don't write that! They are probably not going to like it!

Statistically speaking, you should have at least some empowering events. If a person has more intense destructive associations in his life than empowering associations, he will have more pain than pleasure living which would lead to suicide. You are alive. You have to have some positive believes that keep you going!

Think of a time that you were loved. It can be by a family member, by a friend, or by a teacher. Think of a time that you have done something that you thought were impossible. Maybe there were somethings in your life before that you never thought you would have or accomplish, but there are here now. Can you see any events like that in your life?

Now after all the talks on how to choose your experiences, let's do some real work that will get you choose your material!

Action Step 3

Here is how you can come up with fantastic experiences materials.

There are 2 ways that you can recall experiences like this:
1st method: Most people cannot remember every single detail that happened in their past. They remember certain MOMENTS. There is a good reason for that. Those moments are very likely to be the key moments in their

lives where they made the key neuro-associations (or meanings, as in common language)!

Think back to those moments and try to feel what you felt when you re-live those moments. Close your eyes and recall as many of them as possible. Replay the strongest of them. What do you see? Write them down. Can you concisely discover some of the believes you may formed?

2nd method: Now look at some of the positive activities you do today...sports, community services, helping your friends, etc. Close your eyes and visualize you doing those activities. Feel the feelings you get them. Really feel the joy, the excitement, the love, or whatever the feels good to you. When you really feel it, think back to the past of looking for one experience where you decided to pick up this activity. Why do you do it? What's it like? Can you remember exactly how you flipped the switch in your mind and start doing this positive activity? Write them down.

Magic Bullets for Writing your Essay
Set One

Before we start writing our essay, let's get do the fun part.

You have read patiently through the previous chapters on what colleges want. Now it's time to reward you with some tricks that will transform your essay from an average John to an Iron Man on Steroids.

The techniques below are not your solid content to put down as your materials, but "Magic Bullets" that will make your content MUCH MORE powerful and attractive to the AJs. They are not designed to unethically manipulate the AJ into granting you acceptance. Please use them cautiously and ethically. Let the fun Begin!

Show Don't Tell

How to avoid the #1 mistake students make in their essays to come off as a poser

One of the most common questions colleges ask in both their short answer and essays can be phrased as "what are the qualities/talents you have to describe yourself?" This seems to be a reasonable question when you first look at it. It does sound right that colleges need to know your qualities before they determine if they want to let you in.

However, have you ever heard someone say "I am a good person!", "I am cool!", or "I have a big dick!"? I have.

(By I have, I mean I have heard people like talking about themselves like that. Not the big penis size. Although I am ~~perfectly~~ adequately satisfied with my own size; I am not worried about it at all!!)

What is the first thought that comes to your mind when you hear say that about themselves?

Do you think "Man, He must be the kindest and coolest person I know!"?

No. You think "What a shameless douchebag with a tiny penis!" When students see "what are your qualities?" type of questions, they assume that it is an opportunity to show the school their "qualities". So they wrote down "I am a good person!", "I am honest!", or "I have a big heart!"

...

What do you think readers are going to think?

If you don't like it when you hear someone making a self-promoting talk, the schools don't either.

So why do schools ask you this type of questions?

Schools ask you this type of questions not to blindly believe you, but to judge your real qualities by the way you tell other people about yourself. It's not about WHAT qualities you tell the college, but HOW you describe your qualities.

To my surprise, the old cliché "your actions speak so loudly that we can't hear your words" actually works very well in our context of writing an outstanding CAE.

People believe another person has certain quality based on the actions the person takes; not by what he says. Do you know someone in your life who you KNOW that she/he is a back-stabbing bitch but always says nice things in front of you? They apply to colleges too! Over the years, judges have gotten good at detecting these posers.

So how to you present your qualities so that the AJs will believe that you are not one of those posers?

Here is the technique: If you want the colleges to believe that you are a kind person, instead of start by saying "I AM...", first SHOW them your experience.

Illustration

In season 5 of America's got talent Nathaniel Kenyon's audition (Yes, I am using a TV show as an example), he introduces himself to the judge and the audience by starting saying this:

*"My name is Nathaniel, I am 19 years old from back state Georgia.
I love to sing. I love to play guitar and just express myself through music."*

(Wow! That was a boring, but a typical introduction—and I am not talking just about the TV show here.)

So, the judges start asking questions next.

Howie: what do you do?

Nat: I work at an elderly home.

Howie: You do? Well that's commendable that a young man would find a job where he is serving the community like that. How did you get involved in the (working at elderly home service)?

Nat: Actually last year my grandmother passed away. She lost her fight to Lou Gehrig's Disease. After seeing that and just seeing people being there and helping her, it kinda inspired me to do something like that...at the elderly home I work I sing on Saturday nights...it's therapeutic to them. You can tell them enjoyed it. (Audience cheers)

Howie: What does it mean to you?

Nat: Everything! Music is a way to inspire people and a way that nothing else can! So...(Audience cheers)

Howie: And you want this to be your life?

Nat: More than anything! If I can have this be my life, I can wake up every day...smiling!

If he can turn this into an essay, the experience would have demonstrated his quality without him describing his qualities. In this example, he never once said anything about his quality! But what have we learned about his personal qualities?

He is courageous—he goes against the social norm and works at an elderly home even though he is 19. He is action oriented—he takes actions of dedicating his career and youth to serve what he believes in instead of sitting on his lazy ass like most average Americans...me for example. He gets inspired by good acts—he chose his career because he was positively inspired by kind acts of others. He is extremely passionate about music. (Contrary to teenagers, many adults' passions die later on in life so passion is something that adults find relatively rare among themselves) He is very inspiring. And last but not the least, he is a kind person!

Did Nat put in words saying that "I am incredibly courageous! I am action oriented. I get inspired by good acts. I am passionate. And Oh, I almost forgot to say; I am the kindest person!"? No! If he said that, the judges probably won't let him pass. The audience will probably boo him!

So what is the technique Nat unconsciously used here that impressed the judges that you can use in your college essay?

The technique's name is:

Show Don't Tell

Show Don't Tell is a writing technique of composing a sentence describing an action, observation, or belief which the reader obtains insights of the character.

We gain multiple insights of someone not by that person tells us what kind of person he is, but by interpreting what he says and does. Often we subconsciously interpret meaning of the sentences and we are not even aware of it. But we get a "feel" when we hear those sentences.

If you hear someone say "I am Black", does it raise certain emotions inside of you? But if you hear someone say "I am a n*gger", does that raise a different kind of emotion? Do you immediately form some beliefs you have about a person who said that? You may not be able to consciously describe what your beliefs, but you can feel it when someone says a strong word like "nagger".

Everything you write has an underline meaning.

If the applicant writes "I want to play a bigger game in life."

What do we know (or subconsciously know) about her?

1. To her, life is a GAME.

2. She is doing something on a small scale right now.

3. She wants to do it on a bigger scale.

If someone writes "I push through the last few meters of the competition."

What do we believe about him?

We know that:

1. He is a finisher. He finishes what he starts even though it may be painful.

2. He is the "push himself" type. Not the "pull himself" type. There is a big difference.

3. He functions excellently under pressure such as in a competitive environment.

You don't need to tell the AJ straight up how you perceive life, or you are a finisher. It is much more believable if you SHOW them by the other things you say. That is also a reason why experiences type of essays are generally better materials than other types of essays. You don't tell them who you are or your values. They perceive who you are through your experiences.

If you have talents/outstanding achievements, describe the achievements with concrete numbers. "I run 1000 miles in 11 days.", is much better than saying "I am a genius in long distance running."

When you show your qualities, think about how each sentence you write is going to come off across like. Look for the meanings behind the meanings. Many times your sentence may contain double meaning that can be used to your advantage!

When Nat said "I can wake up every day...smiling." We know that he is both very positive (smiling) and hard working. (Lazy people don't talk about waking up).

Action step

First think back to your experiences illustrating the 5 fundamental qualities. Jog down how you can show the qualities without telling. Compose your sentences into ones that actively demonstrate your qualities, characters, and talents.

Exam your sentences and read between the lines searching for what they really mean. The more you do it, the better you get at writing these "underline meaning sentences".

If the questions are short answers asking for your qualities, tell a story that support your primary quality you want to demonstrate with factual data (how many years, what do you specifically do) and throw in there at least one secondary quality.

Sensory Emersion

The Secret of Instantly Emerging Your Reader Into Your Story

What is the percentage do you think our communication is through words?

95% ?

70% ?

50% ?

The real answer is 7%. Study has shown, 55% of our communication is through our body language and 38% from our voice tones.

This makes sense. Before language has been developed, human had survived for millions of years. Language is only developed 6000 years ago in the human evolution. It is normal to assume that other communication skills such as body language and voice tones are much more developed in the human body.

How a person says the word "Hi" could bring a big difference in how the recipient feels. A person can say "Hi!" in a way that communicates "I like you." A person can say "Hi" and communicate "Fuck off!" Or a person can say "Hi" in a sensual way that excites you. Is it useful to communicate to the AJ with more than just the 7% of words like the average student?

Yes. But I have to communicate words with AJ! He is going to read my essay. It's not like I can just go up to him and say "Hi!" You do only use words to communicate in your essay. However, there is a way that will make the AJ engage your story in ways including all forms of communication!

Studies have shown, a human's mind cannot differ what is real and what he vividly imagines. If you want the AJ to engage in your story on a level that is not just words and feel "real", the key is to make the AJ imagines vividly what happens in your story. Once the AJ vividly imagines events as he reads your essay, he will take in all the communication through all channels as if he is there looking, listening, smelling, touching, and tasting everything.

This technique is called sensory Emersion.

The key is to engage the AJ's 5 senses simultaneously to simulate a trans-state of imaginary experience. Utilizing all 5 sensory descriptions (or at least visual, auditory, and kinesthetic) at the same time creates a subconscious commend that simulates another reality.

If a person receives subconscious comments (such as looking at the word "pink elephant" will make you imagine a pink elephant in your mind regardless of you are willing or not.), he is going to imagine it in his head. When he receives subconscious commends that engage 80% of his senses at the same time, he is going to simulate a reality in his mind that is so vivid that it is as if he is experiencing it for real.

In another word, if you imagine seeing, hearing, smelling, touching, and tasting something/someone, the visual experience in your mind will be so clear that it feels like you are "living" the experience!

Read and compare the below paragraphs:

Paragraph One:

A very old woman tries to stand up from her wheel chair. She tries to say something. But I couldn't make out what she said. She grabs my hand.

Paragraph Two:

Damn! She smells like hospital.
The lines on her faces remind me the 1000 train tracks I saw in Bombay.

She is moving her draw up and down and I feel like that I can almost hear her chewing her invisible food.

Her hands shiver as she slowly stands up from her wheel chair.

She tries to say something in a shaky and week voice but I couldn't comprehend.

Suddenly I thought she was going to fall down for a second! But instead she grabs my arm with her ice cold hands!

Can you feel a difference here? Which paragraph communicates more? Which paragraph left you a deeper impression? Which paragraph gives you more emotions when you read it?

Most students don't know this technique so they write their essay in the first paragraph's style. Even if they do make a sensory description, they only engage one sense! These kinds of essays don't communicate as much as they should. No vivid visualization is formed in the AJ's mind. No emotional exchange. This puts them on a disadvantage.

The second paragraph utilized 4 out of the 5 senses at the same time! (Visual, auditory, smell, and thermal) The last sentence also adds in an additional sixth sense which is your internal feeling. (People identify "feeling" their internal feelings). By engaging multiple senses at the same time, the reader vividly experience what you experienced. The technique is commonly used in hypnosis and Neuro-linguistic Programming. In vastly successful fiction novels such as *Harry* Potter, you will also find the wide use of this technique.

How to use this technique:

The top 3 senses that account for 80% of the communication is visual, auditory, and kinesthetic. Make sure to engage at least the top 3 senses as you describe at key moments of your story. Three example key moments are: the beginning, emotional moments of your story, and the climax of your story. Whenever you want to emerge the AJ into the exact moment in your story or make the AJ experience the exact emotions you want him to experience, use Sensory Emersion.

Action Step:

Write a paragraph of anything, if you don't have anything to write, write about your sexist moment. And practice using sensory hypnotization technique. Engage all 5 senses at the same time and your "internal feeling"! GO

Chapter 5
Killer Introduction

A good essay starts with an excellent introduction.

An excellent essay starts with an outstanding introduction.

An outstanding essay starts with no introduction.

How is that possible!!? We need a punch line that gets the AJ's attention! How can you say that we don't need an introduction?!

Yes! A punch line does grab AJ attention...as long as the rest of the content is as good as the punch line!

Many students put a disproportional amount of energy into writing the introduction and the introduction is truly refreshing and exciting. That is why a good essay has an excellent introduction and an excellent essay has an outstanding introduction. Unfortunately, those students' introduction punch lines become the best part of the whole essay. Everything is downhill where there on (Like a great trailer with a disappointing movie)!

The function of introduction is to lead the AJ into your story.

Imagine the essay itself is a nice dinner. The introduction is the appetizer part of the dinner. The function of the appetizer is to get you to enjoy the main course. If the appetizer is too delicious or taste too strong, the dinner itself won't taste as good. If an appetizer that blends in with the meal perfectly, how great that dinner will be!

A powerful introduction (punch line) serves as a pattern interrupt for the AJ which could be very useful when he is in an "essay reading sleep". However, most of the times when a student uses a punch line introduction, the punch line becomes an attention grabber just for the sake of attention grabbing. It doesn't serve to smoothly deliver the real content. Therefore the intrinsic value of an introduction is lost. What is worse is that *if your introduction doesn't bring the reader into your story, your body paragraphs won't ether.*

Your English teacher didn't teach you that did she?

An outstanding essay's introduction blends perfectly with the story and they become "one". There is no need to "introduce" the story. The introduction itself is so smooth that it serves as a perfect logic step not only grabbing the AJ's attention but also bringing him deeply into the story. If the introduction becomes one with your story, the story can't stand alone without it.

(If you have an introduction already, the easiest way to see if your introduction is ideal is to take it out of the essay, and see if the story changes. If it does, your introduction is not doing an outstanding job.)

There are many ways to produce a killer introduction that is both a punch line and brings the AJ into your story. You can get very creative on this.

I have developed an easy and incredibly effective technique for it inspired by hypnosis techniques. The name of the technique is:

Dream Introduction

Bringing AJ into your story as if bringing them into a dream.

(I know the above name is a bit corny but I will explain)

Have you enjoyed some of your dream?

I have. Some of my dreams gave me quite an experience! (Especially the sexy ones—ok this is a good example of too much information on an official writing!)

When you dream, do you remember how you get to dream environment or do you just "get into" the scenario?

When I dream about being in the middle of a grave yard chased by zombies, I don't remember how I got to the grave yard. I am just "there"! (Unfortunately that doesn't ease the horror followed that whole night!) While I am running like there is no tomorrow from the grave yard in my dream, I really don't give a shit about how I got there at the first place. The experience itself was what I cared about!

Dreams can give you quite an experience without you knowing how to you get to the "being chased by zombies", "in classroom without pants), or "you are lying on your bed but has a cat or demon on top of you and you couldn't move" (Yes, I often times suffer from sleep paralysis). It just gets you straight into the dream.

Therefore, a person's dream has the best introduction. No matter how vivid and intense the dream experience is, you never know how you get there at the first place. Yet you don't care. You are just **in** it. What if you can smoothly bring the AJ in your story as if you are bringing him into a dream— you dream?

That would be slick!

And you are going to learn how to do it.

Most people try to "introduce" the story to the AJ. It is understandable where they are coming from. The AJ doesn't know the situation; she needs to know that the story takes place at the 1st annual Long Beach Cross Country Race in 2015; and there are 12 teams with second division runners...blah blah...(do they really need to know these details?)

So how do most students start their essays? Here is an example:

In the summer 2007 my junior year, I participated in the regional short distance track competition in Long Beach, California. My school was competing with three neighbor schools, Lincoln High, Pasadena High, and Arcadia. They were all top long distance running schools. I ran Junior Varsity in the 3rd division. Before the race, my coach called my name and I got really nervous before the competition…

Wow! Who ~~the hell~~ cares!

A majority of students write their college application essays this way. You see, there is a fill-in-the-blank section of the application where you put statistical information. Essay part of the application is your only chance to show the college "You as a person. Not a number". Take the AJ to your experience! Own her! Bring the AJ to the dream in your CAE and she will bring you to your dream college.

In dreams, the reason that we don't need an introduction is that we never get a report or debrief on what the situation is. We EXPLORE in our dreams. We get thrown into a scenario where we get to know what is going with exploration—even if it sometimes means zombies coming out.

Read the below introduction:

It was noisy. The sound of the runners sprinting on the red rubber track and their ~~fat~~ overweight moms screaming created a particularly disturbing irritation. The competition stadium seemed dark even though the dawn's yellow sunlight burns my forearms like a hundred needles thrusting into my skin. I can smell my own sweet. My mouth is dry. I must be dehydrated.

My coach, a proper nutcase, with his usual freakily brushed long blond hair stands on outside edge of the tracks. He checked several tired teammates from the last wave to see if they were injured. Suddenly he turned his head to my direction and shouted "Shu! Get ready in 5 minutes!

You are up!"

The first thought that came into my mind is

"Fuck!"

The languages are not appropriate enough for college essays, but do you get the idea? I am describing a track competition I participate in as a runner. You can tell what is going on 1 min into the essay. The setting of the story takes you directly into the experience. The AJ knows the setting by what she experiences at the moment and all the clues she gets.

I use the sensory hypnosis to emerge the reader live my story vividly as if it is a live experience. The cues in the environment let reader discover what's going on QUICKLY.

Action Step

Now you have already chosen your material to write, brain storm where you want to start describing your experience and Use the Dream Introduction technique to write a draft of your introduction. Be sure to use sensory hypnotization technique. If you want a bonus, throw in other techniques as well such as The Name Game. Go

Chapter 6
Writing Your Experience

Writing the experience itself

What is the single most important part of a CAE?

The introduction?

The conclusion?

The word choice?

As the AJ reading your essay, what makes the biggest difference is not the number of beautiful words you have or the way you use complex sentence structure. The heart and soul of your essay lies in your content of the experience itself. (Although some people think that SAT vocabulary makes their essay better. They don't. So many people are doing it, it is becoming corny in itself.)

If I use all the techniques you have learned in this book by now, but I have a shitty content, my essay is still shitty. AJs get thousands of essays with beautiful words but empty real story. On the contrast, if you have a solid writing of your experience, even without any techniques, you still have a very good shot.

Real content generates real value. You experience is the main body paragraphs expressing what happens in the event, which revelation you gain, and how you grow.

Correctly and clearly illustrating your experience the single most important factor in optimizing your chance of getting into your dream college.

Most students do not have a clue of how to write their experience.

Really.

Too many students have truly magnificent experiences in their lives but when they put down in their application essay, it sounds mundane and just not the way it should be. Those students lost the chance to get what they deserved—a great college life of their choice. Their lives changed forever for the worse because of that.

But that won't be you! YOU will write the most outstanding experience and knock the judge's socks off! You will GET IN to your Dream College and have a great future of never settling for less!

Let's learn the exact ways to make it happen.

Any experience you have is composed of 3 key components.

Your physiology

Your focus

Your interpretation

Your Physiology

Your physiology is how you and other people move. Let's do a fun experiment! Now smile. Really, smile! Just trust me and do it! It's OK if it's a fake smile. Just keep the facial motion of smiling.

And keep the smile on.

Now I want you to think of the most horrific and depressing experience in your life.

But Keep the smile ON while you do!

While you are thinking about that horrible experience and keeping your fake smile on, try to feel the negative emotions you experienced then.

Try it.

Keep the smile on!

See, you can't feel the negative emotions from your absolute most horrible memories!...as long as you keep the smile on your face...even if it's a fake smile!

Physiology is the number 1 determinant of how you experience anything. Clearly illustrating physiology in your event will communicate exact each character's emotions, internal dialogues, and character shift.

Read the below paragraph,

We stand facing each outside of Delta terminal. The cold wind blew through me but my mind is on something else.

We apart and breathe deeply and slowly. She strikes the back of my right arm with hers. Then she suddenly raises her voice and got very emotional. She tries to say something.

I don't let her finish. My left hand wraps around her neck, pull her in, and my mind goes blank.

In this paragraph, can you see how physiology illustration is able to communicate on a level where pure adjectives such as "wonderful, magnificent, hot, sexy, or loving" cannot nearly describe? Physiology makes your experience the way it is! Also through physiology the reader experience what you experience.

Now, let see another example:

There was a stunk, like a spoiled cheese, passenger next to me, a ~~fat~~ overweight woman sitting on her electric scooter. She looked at me and tried to stand up from her electric scooter. Her hands were on the handle bars and she was trying her best effort to get up. She mumbled something but I couldn't make out what she was saying because her heavy respiration.

Suddenly she grabbed my arm! Oh god her palm was sweaty! She shouted "There is no more battery in my scooter!" (Breathing heavily) "Help me get the Terminal attendant! I need to use the restroom immediately!"

I was in shock to say the least. I looked to my right, the airport restrooms, about 12 feet from where we were. I looked at her. Then I looked at the restroom again. Then I looked at her. She must have noticed me doing so and now have an expression on her face as if my action offended her. But before she could say anything again, her body quickly shivers, a strange sound came from her behind as if a bubble burst, followed by an overwhelming revolting smell.

The reader experience or simply "get" what I experience by illustration of physiology. It is the most direct and fast way to get your reader (AJ) in state. It is an essential part that builds your experience. You HAVE TO include physiology in illustrating your event. Be sure to include how your breathing (the most primal movement) changes as the event unfolds.

Your Focus

Your focus is where you put your attention on.

Let's do another fun experiment! Now look around the room you are in for 5 seconds and look for everything that is brown, GO!

OK, now, without looking, tell me how many pink items did you see?

Any?

You can look around now and find all those pinks you "missed".

The fact is that you did see everything in the room. But because you are only focusing on brown items, what you remember is only the brown items, not the pink ones.

If you go to a party and you focus on people fighting, at the end of the night you will say that the party is very intense! If at the same party you instead focusing on a depressed group of kids sitting in the corner, at the end of night you will say the party sucks! If at the party you focus on the hot opposite girl/guy is giving you signals, even if the party sucks for everyone else, you will think it is a great party!

What you focus on determines what your experience is. Not the environment.

If your essay is supposed to focus on the color pink but you write too much color brown, guess what the AJ will think your essay's color (thesis) is? Most students don't know how to use the power of focus in their essay. They have a punch line for the sake of punch line for their intro, ending with their desired color pink (thesis conclusion), but the main body paragraphs are filled with brown, yellow, green, etc. How distorted does his essay become!

In your essay, while you are describing your experience, you need to put the correct attention to what you are saying. For example, if you are trying to writing an experience where you overcome fear and discovered your true self, you need to focus on everything about you overcoming the fear. Not fear itself.

Read and compare the below experiences:

There she is. The most beautiful dancer of that night. She has long dark curly hair. Her black dress that shows her figure in an attractive yet elegant way. Her face takes everyone man's breathe away. Should I ask her to dance? It is my first time at this dance ball! I only had my first lesson! What should I do? She must think that I am a beginner and won't like dancing with me! What if she rejects me? I don't even know how to properly ask someone to dance! You know what? Screw it! I will just ask her!

There she is. The most beautiful dancer of that night. She has long dark curly hair. Her black dress that shows her figure in an attractive yet elegant way. Her face takes everyone man's breathe away. Should I ask her to dance? It is my first time at this dance ball! I only had my first lesson! The thought of it is already making me sweat! But if I don't ask people to dance with me, I will never be able to learn how to dance.

She is also standing there looking a bit uneased...no one is asking her to dance (Presumably because they were just as nervous)! Despite feeling that I am being suffocated by anxiety, and I may get sick any time, I took a deep breath, with my shaking legs, took the first step towards her.

What's the difference between the 2 paragraphs? They both talk about how you conquered your fear of asking this beautiful and advanced dancer. They are both true. However the first one focuses on the fear. But the second one focuses on CONQUERING the fear.

Even though both paragraphs can describe your experience honestly, the first paragraph just isn't powerful on illustrating what you want to say. The second one doesn't deviate from its focus. It keeps the reader intact with the thesis direction you want to lead them to. (Conquering the fear)

Your interpretation

The experience you have can be as rare as working with scientists in NASA, or as common as getting in a fight with your mother. However at the end of the day, WHAT HAPPENED doesn't matter. What matters the most is "what does this mean to you?"

Working with NASA can mean "it's just a summer internship" and Fighting with mom can be "the bonding experience with my most intimate family member which in turn I learned a life lesson."

Have you ever done something together with a friend and you guys had the exact same experience, but the experience means totally different things to you guys? People may have the same experience, but the ultimate difference the experience brings to the person is not WHAT the happened, but what it means to the person.

In our previous Tony Robbins example, Tony and his dad had the exact same experience! Someone delivered food to their family. However that experience is extremely empowering for Tony and extremely disempowering for his dad.

When the AJ reads your experience, the ultimate goal is to learn about you by how you react and interpret your special experience. Most students spend almost all portion of the text describing their experience. Few of them ever really write about what exact this experience mean to them. They are too busy writing about the experience itself.

How does interpretation work?

To interpret something means, we first have to ask ourselves questions.

If I don't ask myself "Why did that girl see my face, scream 'Gross!' and run the other way?" I won't get my interpretation of "Because I am too good-looking that she got embarrassed."

We ask ourselves questions every day. Questions like "Should I snooze?" "Does he/she like me?", "Why am I such a loser?"

The quality of your life is determined by the quality of questions you ask yourself. Everything you experience, you ask questions as it is happening as well as when the event is over.

When you ask yourself a question, your brain will look for the answer. Once you create the answer for the question you ask, it becomes your belief. During your key moments in life, you asked some very special questions that affect your belief systems therefore your actions ever since. Questions such as "Why does this happen to me?" OR "Why does this happen **for** me?"

The flow of your experience goes:

Event happening (your physiology and your focus determines what you experience) -> Ask yourself a question (your question determines the interpretation of what the event means) -> Create the answer/form a new revelation/belief that you will take action upon

Your interpretation is what question you ask yourself and what Answer/meaning you create. That is the key to your experience. By illustrating your interpretation of your experience, you are able to program the AJ to simulate your exact psychological experience of the event.

Read the following example:

As we walk to the front section of the dance floor, I can feel other people start staring at us. "I am Jessica." She smiles. "I am Shu." I replied. Her perfume is intoxicating.

The music starts.

I put my right arm on her back (wow!). We began dancing in front of the crowd. It is at this moment, I realized we are the first and only people dancing while everyone is watching.

Darn! I can't believe this is actually happening! I am actually dancing front of everyone! I don't know how she is enjoying the dance but I am struggling with the 2 moves I learned from class today. Somehow I am managing to move with the music and not stepping on her which is a victory for me.

Just as I am enjoying this victory, suddenly thoughts start flying into my mind. Is she bored dancing with me? I am only a beginner! Am I good enough? I suddenly start panicking and messing up my moves (even though I only know 2 of them)

I babble to her ears nervously "I am only a beginner. I just had my first lesson today! Are you enjoying the dance?" As I speak, I am already making anticipated responses from her. She must be going to bush me off by saying "No. I am fine. I am enjoying it." To my surprise, instead she leans her head in and really listens to what I say until I finish!

Jessica looks into my eyes, and smiles. Then she leans next to my ears, and says in a soft voice "You reminded me the first time I learned dancing. Shu, you have to start somewhere!" Then she pulls back, looks at me, and smiles again.

I feel a sudden jolt in my body. It feels like that the room just got brighter! Right! I finally understand! No matter where I am, I don't need to be perfect to start. I need to start somewhere! And not just in dancing.

I can start taking on classes that seemed very difficult to challenge myself! I can start volunteering at the neighborhood retirement home and not wait for the "perfect time"! And I can start reconnecting with people in my life whom I have had a less than perfect relationships".

In this paragraph, as I am narrating me dancing with Jessica, I also include my thought process through the event. I ask questions of what each happening means to me "Is she bored? Am I good enough?" Also I interpret what each happening means to me such as "this is a victory for me".

At the climax of the story when she gave me the revelation of "Shu, You have to start somewhere." I interpret what this experience means to me. It means *"No matter where I am, I don't need to be perfect to start. I need to start somewhere! And not just in dancing.*

I can start taking on classes that seemed very difficult to challenge myself! I can start volunteering at the neighborhood retirement home and not wait for the "perfect time"! And I can start reconnecting with people in my life whom I have had a less than perfect relationships".

Action Step

Now utilize the 3 key factors "your physiology", "your focus" and "your interpretation", write down your experience. Do not go to the next chapter until you finish writing down your experience. Go!

Chapter 7
Growth

Now you have illustrated what happened in your experience and what new empowering believes you formed through this experience, it's time to show AJ the real deal—how you grew from this experience!

Growth is a change of behavior.

Recall the Choose Your Material Chapter, once you make a new neuro-association, your future behaviors will change accordingly.

If a person goes through an event and his behaviors stay the same, he hasn't grown at all. The AJ wants to see how you have grown long-term from your significant experience. If you show the AJ an experience that blows his mind, but you don't show how you have grown from that, it will just become a one-time experience you had, not a long-lasting behavior change which you have grown from.

So the *complete* diagram of your experience goes like this

Event happening (your physiology and your focus determines what you experience) -> Ask yourself a question (your interpretation of what the event means) -> Find/make up an answer (form a new revelation/belief that you will take action upon)-> Growth (how you behave differently after the experience)

To demonstrate how you have grown from the experience, we need to tie your beliefs from this experience to your new behaviors or achievements.

Read the below paragraph example for the dance essay.

The next morning, the first thing I did was registering for a dance class, followed by registering for AP Calculus class for the next semester, it would be my first AP class ever. I signed up for volunteer after school, then I called my dad.

Of course, dancing became my biggest hobby. For the next 6 months, I intensely trained my dancing 6 hours a day, 4 days a week at dance schools. I went to international salsa congresses in San Francisco, Boston, and New York. Through my dance journey, I made friends and mentors all over world from PHD electric engineer from MIT to the founder of a highly respected mutual fund group.

Calculus class turned out to be especially challenging. However I grew to like it and actually got a "5" on the test! It was the start of me taking on 4 more AP classes.

The volunteering experience provided to be especially rewarding. The residences were always delighted to see me every Thursday afternoon. We chat and most of them talked to me about their past and their families. I performed dance routines at the retirement home prior to every formal performance or competition. They applaud very hard every time I do.

I called my dad and he was initially surprised. But soon he was more used to chatting with me on a regular basis. Then my brother and sisters started talking to him. Finally my mom began talking to him. Even though she said they have "a lot of work to do", I have to say that the fact they started talking to each other again shocked us all.

Jessica became my girlfriend...No. She was married to a Marine and shortly moved for their military relocation. We did see each other again 2 years later at a dance conference in San Francisco and talked about that dance.

Prior to the dance, I often feared that I was not good enough; and if I was not good enough, I won't be loved. So I had to be perfect. Today, I still fear that I am not enough at times. But I know that I am loved, and everything will be OK. I don't need to be perfect, no one is. All I need to do is start somewhere, and take the first step.

You can also only focus on ONE aspect of the growth, the main aspect that related to your event. See this example:

The next morning, I joined the salsa training first thing in the morning. For the next 6 months, I intensely trained my salsa dancing 6 hours a day, 4 days a week at dance schools. I went to international salsa congresses in San Francisco, Boston, and New York. Through my dance journey, I made friends and mentors all over world from PHD electric engineer from MIT to the founder of a highly respected mutual fund group.

But the most satisfying part of dancing and travelling is not winning the competition, performing, or connecting with people I have never dreamed of meeting.

It is the moment when I danced with a little girl name Anya from Russia, she asked me if she could dance as beautifully as I do, and I told her that she could be the best and most beautiful dancer in the world. And her eyes light up like Christmas lights!

It is the moment when I danced with an old grandma and told her she is still young and beautiful. And she laughed like a little girl!

It is the moments when I dance with first timers just like when I first started and reassure them to not be afraid and take the first step! And every one of them had a blast!

Jessica became my girlfriend…No. She was married to a Marine and shortly moved for their military relocation. We did see each other again 2 years later at a dance conference in San Francisco and talked about that dance.

Prior to the dance, I often feared that I was not good enough; and if I was not good enough, I won't be loved. So I had to be perfect. Today, I still fear that I am not enough at times. But I know that I am loved, and everything will be OK. I don't need to be perfect, no one is. All I need to do is start somewhere, and take the first step.

Can you see how I tie my new behaviors to my revelation of the experience? I align all my new behaviors and achievements to the experience so that the experience is a positive game changer in my life.

Action Step

Write down your growth utilizing the structures you learned in this chapter. As a bonus you can use the tricks on how to write your achievements to tie your accomplishments to the experience. GO!

Chapter 8
Ending: Call for Action

Most students' CAE will end here. They end their CAEs at the Growth stage.

That is good.

But not good enough.

Your CAE is not just an essay you turn into your English teacher. It is your COLLEGE APPLICATION ESSAY. It has a specific purpose. The purpose is to get you into that dream college of yours.

So what do you do when you are facing the person who can grant your acceptance?

It's simple. You ask her to grant you acceptance.

What??!! Really!? Isn't that a little bit... I don't know.

If a teacher gives a confusing lecture, but she doesn't ASK the class if anyone has questions, how many students do you think is going to raise their hands and say "I don't understand a thing that came from your month!"?

If a sales person gives an amazing sales pitch, but he doesn't ASK the prospect to buy the product, how many customers do you think is going to proactively buy the product?

It is easy to ignore someone you don't really like but you know that he/she likes you. It is much harder to refuse going out on a date with him/her if they ASKS you.

Your essay may really demonstrate to the AJ that you are an unbelievable person and she should let you in. But she may not make up her mind just yet. There may be too many other applicants or the AJ may start to over think.

When you ask her straight up to let you in, it is a jolt to her and it psychologically force her to make an immediate decision—right after reading that amazing essay of yours.

The result is unquestionable.

If you enjoy the visualization exercise we did before. You can imagine you are the AJ and just finishing reading an amazing essay from an application.

Imagine first scenario where the student just ends essay without asking you to accept her. Try to reject her. Imagine the second scenario where the student ends her amazing essay by asking you "Dear AJ, Would you help me in my journey to achieve and contribute my gift to the world by accepting me to my dream college, _____ College?" Try to reject her.

It is much harder to reject the second student isn't it?

By directly asking the AJ to grant you acceptance in your essay, you not only demonstrate great interest in his school, but also makes her almost impossible to reject you.

How you ask at the end can be very creative. Using the dance example, I can write:

I learned from that one dance that often times I will be insecure, fearful and not perfect. But all I need to do is to start somewhere—take the first step, metaphorically and literally. I apply it to anything I do: dance, school, and family. I cannot repay Jessica for her help and generosity; I can only pay forward this blessing another person. I will sing to them the words they have been craving from someone for too long. "You are enough. You have always been enough. And you will always be. All you need is to start somewhere, and your dream will follow."

Dear Admissions Staff, my dream is to spend the next 4 years of my life in _____ University. So what is your answer? Can you help me starting the next stage of my life here, at _____ University?

It takes someone blood made of ice to say no to that.

Get creative with your ways of asking. I am sure you had thousands of ways to ask your parents what you want since you were a kid. Just use the best ones on the AJ.

Action Step

Play with your endings, be creative and write a 5 ways you can ask the AJ for your acceptance. Choose the best one and elaborate on it. Make it really good. GO!

Magic Bullets for Writing your Essay
Set two

The Good Looks

Instantly Make Your Essay Look Better Without Adding a Single Word

Yes. I am serious. It is possible. And it requires almost no effort on your part.

The easiest way that will instantly make your essay look better without using a single word is to structure the paragraphs in your essay so it looks pleasing to the eyes.

Look at the below paragraph. How do you feel?

An example of a neuro-association is: Ducks associate the first thing they see as its mother. There is a real story of a male duck saw a Jeep when it was first born, so it thought the Jeep was its mother. It chased jeeps every time it saw one to get motherly care. When it was an adult and ready to mate, it would try to mate with Jeeps! The experience is: a baby duck saw a jeep when it was first born. The association is: Mother=Jeep. The habitual actions are: "trying to get mother care from Jeeps, and trying to mate with Jeeps." Just like the duck, human make critical neuro-associations at very moments in our experiences that shapes our future behaviors. Many of them happen to us at a very young age without our conscious control. But they also happen later in life (especially when you are a teen). There are only a few of these experiences and they tend to be very emotional. However, our experiences are not as obvious as the ones we see in ducks. And because we are not consciously aware, we don't notice the impact they have on our lives.

Now look at the same content below with a different line structure.

An example of a neuro-association is: Ducks associate the first thing they see as its mother. There is a real story of a male duck saw a Jeep when it was first born, so it thought the Jeep was its mother. It chased jeeps every time it saw one to get motherly care. When it was an adult and ready to mate, it would try to mate with Jeeps!

The experience is: a baby duck saw a jeep when it was first born.

The association is: Mother=Jeep.

The habitual actions are: "trying to get mother care from Jeeps, and trying to mate with Jeeps."

Just like the duck, human make critical neuro-associations at very moments in our experiences that shapes our future behaviors. Many of them happen to us at a very young age without our conscious control. But they also happen later in life (especially when you are a teen).

There are only a few of these experiences and they tend to be very emotional. However, our experiences are not as obvious as the ones we see in ducks. And because we are not consciously aware, we don't notice the impact they have on our lives.

Can you feel how much better the exact same content feels now? The first one really gave me stress when I read it! (And I am the one who wrote it!) The second one is much more relaxing and I can actually take in the information.

If a good tasting cheese cake literally looks like someone's diarrhea, even if someone tastes it, the taster won't say it's as good as it could be (if they even taste it at all). But an average tasting cheese cake that looks absolutely delicious could really make the taster say "Wow! This is amazing!"

Even if a student may have great content for his essay, he won't get as much credit as he deserves than students who don't have as good contents but the structure looks beautiful and easy to understand.

Structuring your essay so it looks please to the eyes is very important. Not only it is beautiful to the eyes, the shape of the structure also makes the content most receptive to brains. Human uses a large amount of spatial perception in cognitive function. The space between the lines literally helps a person to take in the content itself. A huge pile of text is a turn off. Beware of the structure of your essay.

Languages Pre-approves You to College

Trigger words that prequalify you to the colleges

I went to high school in South Pasadena, California. In my "hood", we developed our own language such as "Yo! sup?!","Dude", "Peace Out", and "Bro".

One day, some stranger approached my group and said "Greetings! Isn't it such a wonderful sunny afternoon!? How do you do?"

Naturally we replied him politely "Fuck off, pedophile!". However, if he would have approached my group and said, "Yo! What's up guys! Dude where is the bathroom?"

We would probably reacted to him better and tell him the way to the restroom, maybe even not to report him to our security!

What is illogical is, "Greetings! Isn't it such a wonderful sunny afternoon!? How do you do?" is a perfectly polite way to saying hello to strangers! On the other hand, the sentence "Yo! What's up guys?!" is composed with words that are not commonly found in the academic dictionary.

So what made us to give totally different reactions to two strangers?

The reason is when the guy who came up to us and said "Greetings! Isn't it such a wonderful sunny afternoon!? How do you do?" A voice screams in our heads "DANGER PEDOPHILE DANGER!"

But when the guy who came up and said "Yo! What's up guys?!" We hear that he uses **language that we use**, so we automatically assume that he is ONE OF US.

If you are applying for a professional school such as business schools or medical schools, the people in that school have a set of language they use. They may be words or abbreviations such as ROA, net investment, ROI, etc.

Each different campus has its own different interesting slang words that relate to their campus.

When a group of people all uses certain words that others don't normally use, they identify themselves as a group. If you use language that people in certain group uses, they will subconsciously assume you are ONE OF THEM. When they feel that you are one of their students, it is emotionally much harder to reject you because it would subconsciously feel like kicking an existing student out!

While the AJ is reading your essay, if the he feels that you are already sound like someone from his college, do you think you will have a much higher chance to get into that college?

But I am not in that college yet and I don't know how to talk like them! You don't have to. Believe or now, when I speak to my friends, we don't only say "Sup dude!" We talk normally just like the pedophile guy. We use less than 1% of our language that is specially communicated among us. Which means that you don't need to know how to talk in sentences in their manner, all you need to do to demonstrate you are part of them is to use a few words that they use. They are called the *Identification Words*.

In our case, the identification words are "Sup", "Bro", "Yo". Those words produce the 80% of the bonding. In your dream college's case, the people there also only use a few words from that culture to identify themselves. Research online, or ask the current students about them. They will know!

Action Step:

Find the top 3 identification words used in your dream college. Write them down below. Use online research, or just ask current students or alumni what are some of the unique words they use in that school.

The Name Game

How to make the College admission judge remember you through your essay instead of coming off across as another pile of application papers

Most College Admission judges (AJ) read hundreds of essays per day. After the first 4 hours of essays reading, do we expect that the judge is still capable of telling the difference between you and the other pile of the 70 essays?

Reading essays after essays, the judge's brain is scrambled like an egg! Not only can he no longer actively try to build report with you through your essay and search for your uniqueness, after reading so many different versions application essays, the judges will be so overwhelmed by all the essays that he would be confused whose experience is who's at the end!

Is it important to distinct yourself from the pile of application paper?

"Yes" would be an understatement.

To have a fair shot at your college application and get your essay the attention it deserves, it is critical to distinct yourself and MAKE SURE the judge remembers your name as a live individual instead of another piece of application paper.

So how exactly do we do that?

Read and compare the below 2 paragraphs:

(1) When she crossed the sidewalk on her way to the church, my big dog noticed her and started walking towards her. She shouted at me from across the street "Is that cute dog yours?"

(2) When she crossed the sidewalk on her way to the church, my big dog noticed her and started walking towards her. She shouted at me from across the street "Warren! Is that cute dog yours?"

What is the difference between the above two paragraphs?

Right! The second paragraph has the Warren's NAME in it! It is no longer just some application paper's experience anymore. It is Warren's experience! Can you feel the difference that by just adding a name, the second paragraph became much more personal? By repeatedly read your name throughout the essay, the AJ vividly experiences your essay through you—"Warren" instead of the faceless "I" that represents everyone else!

When people receive subliminal message, they automatically see it in their mind. The classic example is if you close your eyes and say to yourself out loud "I am not going to imagine a pink elephant", you automatically see a pink elephant.

By the time AJ is done reading most applicants' essays, he has long forgotten their names from the fill-in-the blank section of the college application. But by adding your name in the essay; you are doing the subliminal trick to the AJ's Brain. When AJ sees your name in the essay (preferably more than once), He will automatically visualize a made up version of you. To him, you are no longer just another cold and statistical application paper like the rest competing students. You become a live person who he imagines for the rest of the essay as well as the rest application he reviews!

No matter if the image in judge's mind represents you or not, it's always better to have an image than NOTHING. It becomes much harder to reject you once the AJ had participated a virtual experience through your essay with "you".

In your essay, there are 3 possible places that adding your name would be the most effective.

The first possible place to introduce your name is at the introduction. If you have a powerful introduction that makes the AJ "wake up" for a second from the "essay reading sleep" (ERS), it would be good to put the name there. When the introduction gives a refreshing eye-catching excitement, the judge is likely to remember your name once he sees it...just like you are likely to remember the name of a product if the 30 second commercial is eye catching.

The second place to put your name is at the beginning of the main body paragraph. If your introduction does not suite to introduce your name, the second possible place is at the beginning of your story. (If your story's length is 10 in scale where 1 is the beginning of the story and 10 is the end, this would be around point 2)

AJ at this point is just "warmed up" for your essay and started really getting into the story he is about to experience. Now it is time to make sure to bring him to your journey with you–"Warren".

As the story unfold, the judges will experience a variety of emotions (If you wrote the essay right) like a roller coaster ride! Adding your name at the beginning part of the story will help the AJ associate all the good feelings with "you"!

The third place to put your name is during the climax of your story. The climax is likely to be near point 7 on a 10 scale essay. All the pervious parts of the essay are built up for the climax of the story. During the climax, the AJ should experience the most intense emotion! During that state, seeing your name will make the AJ deeply associate "you" with the emotional roller coaster ride he just had. If you put your name at the beginning of the essay, your name at point 7 out of 10 also serves as a reminder to the AJ.

The Name Game technique will force the AJ to remember you like no other essays he read. Even if he rejects you at first, while he is reading other essays, he will feel your name keeps lingering in his head so he had just go back and accept you! No kidding.

It is preferred to put your name in your essay twice. You may or may not choose to use an eye-catching entrance. It works either way to put your name in the first or second place. You should, however, at least put your name twice and do use your name during the climax of the story.

Do not put your name in the essay by introducing yourself. "Hi! My name is Emma!". "Bye, my name is Emma". There are a variety of ways that will fit your name naturally in the essay which we will talk about later in the book.

If you have a memorable nick name, it is better to use that nick name because it brings up more emotions and it's more personal…and for admission purposes, you want to get personal with the Ad, don't you?

There are countless ways to fill your name naturally in your essay. This is part that you can be creative! I will share 3 ways here for my fellow lazy minds:

1. Have other people say your name

Easy enough. For example, if you have a contribution story, when the person thanks you at the end, you can through in your name there "Elizabeth, Thank you for being in my life." If it's a bonding story, you can through your name there at the emotion exchange "I love you mom" "I love you, Warren, my son"

2. Say your name in your internal dialogues

We all have internal dialogues. It is the voice that speaks to us. If you describe your internal dialogue during key moments, you can easily throw your name in there "I shouted to myself 'Matt, I know you can do it!'"

3. Using External Objects

If you are doing an activity such as community service, you are likely to have a name tag. If you are in a big competition, your name can be on the certificate you received. You can simply describe the external object. "My name 'Jason' is written on the name tag in blue.", or "Seeing my name "Jen" on the certificate of the junior detective award, I feel..."

Last Words

Congratulations! You have now finished this book and have more knowledge on writing CAE than 99.9% of all competing students. Use these knowledge and techniques will make you very powerful—in your college application and in life. I have one last thing I want to say to you personally.

You are meant to be great.

You will become the person that you dreamed to be.

You can and will succeed in life.

In the end, no one can judge you. Not the AJ, not me, not even your parents. Only you can judge yourself by judging the standards you have.

Anything you want in life, YOU will be the one to acquire it! Can you see that dream college life you envisioned again and again in your mind? That is yours.

Now Go Out And Get It!

PS: I am very glad that you finished until the end! Do you know that only 10% of people finish the book they bought? Thank you for taking your time to read my book and take charge of your future! One more key in applying, you should always apply early decision with your dream school. With your top choices schools, apply the early actions (if they have any) instead of regular deadlines. In the early stage, the AJs are not inundated with applications yet so you have a higher chance to get accepted. This also applies for applying to colleges in general. The earlier you apply, the more space there is. Instead if you apply at the last second, you are fighting very few spots with all the other procrastinators who squeezed in their application at the last second too!

Acknowledgement

I want to start by thanking my parents who have always been supportive to me.

Thank you Eben Pagan for all your teaching.

Thank you Warren Buffet for opening my eyes.

Thank YOU, reader. I know this book has brought you something.

Thank you Erin Connery and Ashley Collins.

Thank you Jason Whaling.

Made in the USA
Columbia, SC
11 December 2018